HOW
Full
IS YOUR
BUCKET?

YOUNG READER'S EDITION

HOW Full IS YOUR BUCKET?

YOUNG READER'S EDITION

by TOM RATH and AUDRA WALLACE

Scholastic Inc.

Table of Contents

. . . .

Your Invisible Bucket

Imagine this. Right now, floating above your head, is an invisible bucket. Your classmates, friends, and family members have one, too.

Now picture this. These buckets are constantly emptied or filled, depending on what others say or do to us. When our bucket is full, we feel great. When it's empty, we feel awful.

Each of us also has an invisible dipper. When we use that dipper to fill other people's buckets—by saying or doing things to make them feel noticed and appreciated—we also fill our own bucket.

But when we use that dipper to dip from others' buckets, we actually harm them and ourselves. Bucket dipping is when you do or say something to or about someone that is hurtful—or when you neglect to do something that would have filled someone else's bucket.

Every drop in that bucket makes us stronger, happier, and more confident. But an empty bucket brings us down and makes us feel alone. Every time someone dips from our bucket, it hurts us.

So we have a choice every moment of every day: We can fill each other's buckets, or we can dip from them. It's an important choice— one that affects your health and happiness, and the people around you, in a big way.

CHAPTER 1

Take the Lead

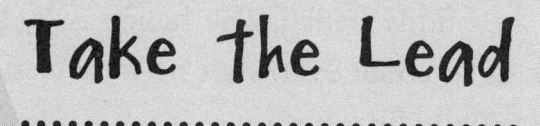

What are some ways to fill a bucket? It can be as simple as a smile and saying hello to someone. Or it can be a big idea that fills a bunch of buckets at once.

Students at a school in Connecticut found a way to do both. They painted a "buddy bench" and message-bearing rocks to inspire happiness and goodwill among their classmates. Fifth grader Clare came up with the idea of getting a buddy bench for her school. She heard about a similar idea on the news. Kids who are feeling lonely or sad can sit on the buddy bench. The bench is a signal to other kids to come over, start up a conversation—and essentially fill a bucket.

"I thought it'd be cool to do it at our school because sometimes, kids, they feel like they don't have friends here, and I wanted that problem to stop," Clare told reporter Ben Lambert at the New Haven Register. *"If I was upset and I was sitting down there, and someone came to help me, I would feel so much better. I know that the smallest memories—that*

person would remember it for a long time."

Her classmate Amelia had an idea, too. She had seen rocks with inspirational messages painted on them, like "You are special." They had made her smile. Amelia wanted to share that feeling with the school.

"Some people may be going through things at home or at school that may upset them, and to find a rock may make them feel better," said Amelia. *"Everyone deserves to feel special."*

Clare and Amelia both brought these ideas into their schools to spread kindness and hope. They recognized how simple words and actions can be uplifting, and they wanted others to do the same. This is the heart of meaningful bucket-filling. Each interaction we have with others gives us the chance to shine a light where sometimes there is none. The best part is that you can start right now.

SIMPLE WAYS
TO FILL A BUCKET:

- Write a note to a friend to let them know you're thinking of them.

- Ask someone to teach you how to do an activity that he or she is really good at.

- Stick up for someone who is being made fun of.

- Invite someone who is sitting alone to join you for lunch or hang out with you at recess.

- Listen to a friend who is having a bad day.

- Ask a person by what name *they* like to be called.

- Hold the door open for someone.

- Help someone clean up a mess.

- Compliment someone.

- Say thank you.

- Smile!

Every time you fill someone's bucket, you're setting something in motion. Think about it. If you fill two buckets a day, and the owners of those two buckets go on to fill two new buckets, more than a thousand buckets will have been filled at the end of ten days.

So continue the chain: When someone fills your bucket, accept it—never just brush off what that person is doing. Fill their bucket in return by saying thank you and letting them know that you appreciate the compliment or recognition. Find a way to compliment and recognize them, too. In turn, you are more likely to share your positive energy with others.

WHAT'S IN YOUR BUCKET?

Think about the bucket-filling moments you've experienced in your life. Write about them below.

Describe a time when someone filled your bucket. How did it make you feel?

_____

_____

_____

_____

_____

_____

_____

_____

_____

Describe a time you filled someone's bucket. How did that person react?

_____

_____

_____

_____

_____

_____

_____

_____

_____

_____

_____

_____

_____

Describe a time when someone dipped from your bucket. How did it make you feel?

_____

_____

_____

_____

_____

_____

_____

_____

_____

_____

_____

_____

_____

Describe a time you dipped from someone's bucket. How did that person react? How do you think that person felt?

_____

_____

_____

_____

_____

_____

_____

_____

_____

_____

_____

CHAPTER 2

Ditch the Dipping

There are many ways that kids *dip* from each other's buckets. Making someone feel left out on purpose is one of them. Mia* knows that feeling very well.

> *"At school, some of the students in my class were laughing and whispering about me behind my back,"* said Mia. *"Then they started ignoring me at recess. I felt left out."*

One way that Mia dealt with the problem was by reaching out to other kids who were being excluded.

> *"A couple of kids told a girl that she couldn't be in their group,"* said Mia. *"So I asked her to be in my group."*

What Mia experienced is called exclusion. Experts say that exclusion is one of the meanest ways that kids bully each other. Its purpose is to make a kid feel like he or she is alone and has no friends.

Being left out isn't an issue just for Mia. Studies

show that one in every six kids is purposely excluded at school. Exclusion is one of the top three ways kids are bullied. Name-calling and spreading rumors are the other two.

Bullying is any unwanted, aggressive behavior that makes someone feel ashamed, excluded, or threatened on purpose. A bully's goal is to be in charge or have power over someone. He or she often uses an angry or aggressive tone of voice, physical strength, embarrassing information, or popularity to harm others. This behavior is often repeated over time in an attempt to hurt someone.

Playful teasing is different from bullying. It's a way of communicating with your friends. It's not meant to harm or control anyone. You and your friend may say funny things about each other for laughs, correct each other's behavior, or encourage each other to get better at an activity. For example, your friends might joke about the silly shirt your mom made you wear to school, and you think it's silly, too. But if the teasing becomes hurtful and you ask your friend to stop, a good friend will stop.

Sometimes playful teasing can get out of control

and become bullying. This can happen if the teasing becomes mean-spirited and is done over and over to the same person. So think before you speak, and be mindful of other people's feelings. There's a popular rhyme that goes, "Sticks and stones may break my bones, but words will never hurt me." But the reality is that words *do* hurt.

• •

Consider your most recent words and actions. Did you . . .

💧 Purposely try to exclude someone?

💧 Poke fun at someone for the way they look or feel, especially in front of others?

💧 Brag about an event that you were invited to but your friend or sibling wasn't?

💧 Talk about a friend behind his or her back?

• •

If so, try to push the "pause" button in your head next time. Think about why you did it.

Sometimes kids dip from other kids' buckets to try to fill their own. They may be the ones who desperately want to fit in or be recognized. For example, some kids might boast about their achievements to overshadow someone else's. Or they might point out what another kid is doing wrong to make themselves feel better about their own weaknesses.

Once you've successfully taken control of your own bucket-dipping, encourage similar changes among those around you. Are your friends always criticizing or mocking others? Do you ever notice them teaming up and "group dipping" from someone's bucket? The next time you see bucket-dipping in progress, do something about it.

Be the kid who *builds up* other kids instead of tearing them down.

Be the kid who cheers other kids on instead of one-upping them.

Speak up and fill someone's bucket instead.

Think Before You Text

Another way kids empty each other's buckets is through texting and posting on social media, like Instagram and Snapchat. Some experts say that kids should hold off on owning digital devices until they are at least fourteen years old. But kids who are much younger are using smartphones, tablets, and other digital devices more than ever. A recent study by Common Sense Media showed that almost half of US kids have their own digital devices by the time they turn nine. They use them to view videos, post photos, play games, and chat with their friends.

If you're using these devices to talk with your buddies, remember that texts can hurt or embarrass others. They can also be misunderstood. Oftentimes you won't be able to gauge another kid's reaction to a comment because you can't see them smile or frown. Plus, it's easy for people to share texts and photos with other people without your knowledge.

If you and your friends are chatting through digital devices, including video games, experts suggest asking yourself these questions before you send a text or post an online comment:

- Would I say this to someone in person?
- Are my words helpful or hurtful?
- Would a parent or other adult approve?

TAKE CHARGE OF YOUR DIPPING

Read the scenarios on the following pages. Then write what you could have done instead.

Scenario #1:

Your friend rushes over to you to share that he finally scored a goal at his soccer game. You interrupt his story to brag about how you scored three goals at your game. What could you have done instead?

_____

_____

_____

_____

_____

_____

_____

Scenario #2:

You and your friends are playing a video game at your house. Your younger brother wants to join in. He keeps coming over and asking to play, but you say no and tell him to stop bothering you. He starts saying silly words and poking you. You start calling him an annoying little baby and tell him to go away. Your friends start calling him that, too. He starts crying. What could you have done instead?

_____

_____

_____

_____

_____

_____

_____

_____

Scenario #3:

On the school bus, you and your friends start making fun of a first grader's hairstyle. At first the younger kid laughs. But then you notice tears forming in her eyes. Your friends keep cracking jokes about her. You sit quietly and ignore them. What could you have done instead?

_____

_____

_____

_____

_____

_____

_____

_____

Scenario #4:

In gym class, one student is never picked for a team. Most kids either choose their close friends or kids they know are good at the activity. You and some of your classmates moan and roll your eyes when the student gets put on your team. What could you have done instead?

_____

_____

_____

_____

_____

_____

_____

_____

_____

Scenario #5:

During a math lesson, you notice that your classmate is struggling with a word problem. He turns to you and asks for help. After all, you scored 100 percent on the last test. You say, "That is so easy! I can't believe you don't know that!" What could you have done instead?

_____

_____

_____

_____

_____

_____

_____

_____

_____

CHAPTER 3

Be a True Friend

· ·

Think about your closest friends. How did you meet them? What made you form a friendship with them? What makes them good friends?

For some kids, making friends isn't easy. Take Rafael, for example. Amanda noticed that he was eating lunch by himself. He was new to the school and barely ever spoke. When she tried to introduce herself, she learned that Rafael spoke only Spanish. He had recently moved to the US from another country. Amanda noticed that Rafael seemed lonely. He kept to himself in class and at recess. Because of the language barrier, he had a hard time making friends. Amanda wanted him to feel included. She used a translating program to write Rafael a note in Spanish. In the note, she invited him to sit with her at lunch and to play with her at recess. Soon they became good friends—and learned to speak each other's languages.

> *"Look for the new kid or the kid who doesn't have a friend, and be that friend,"* Amanda says. *"Everyone needs a buddy!"*

Like Amanda, be the kid who notices when others are in need and reaches out to them. Rafael was a new student who was also struggling with learning a new language. But most of the kids you may want to reach out to have been going to school with you for a long time—you probably just haven't noticed them. Maybe they haven't been in any of your classes or activities. Or you're used to hanging out with your own group of friends and haven't paid attention to who is being ignored and left out.

Here are some ways to be an "includer":

- Scan the room you're in. Look for someone who might need a friend. Walk up and simply say hi.

- Introduce yourself with a smile.

- Introduce him to your group of friends.

- Invite her to hang out with you during recess or another activity.

- Ask him about his interests. Try to remember

what you learned in future conversations with him. This will help you fill his bucket later on in a meaningful way.

• •

Know that sometimes your acts of kindness will not be returned, and the kids you reach out to may not be interested in becoming your friend. They may be shy, nervous, or even wary of your intentions. It takes time to build trust and develop a friendship. But more times than not, when you reach out, you'll be filling a bucket that's desperately in need of some drops.

LEND AN EAR

Whether you're meeting new kids or hanging out with old friends, listening is a huge part of being a true friend. Sometimes when your buddy is talking, you may feel the urge to interrupt her to give advice or talk about a similar problem you're having. But your friend may just want to talk to let out her feelings and frustrations. It's important to let her have her say and be heard. You can show that you're listening by asking questions to help guide your friend toward a solution or by asking what she needs to feel better.

How to be a true friend to your peers:

- Support them in their activities and dreams.

- Be the person they can go to for a kind word and a helpful opinion.

- Recognize their achievements.

- Stand up for them, even when they're not around.

- Be honest with them. You need to be willing to step up and say something if your friend's safety or the safety of others is at risk.

You deserve "true friends," too. Here's how you'll know them:

- They motivate you to accomplish your goals.

- They share common interests with you but expose you to new ones, too.

- They stand up for you, even when you're not around.

- They give you a boost when you're feeling down.

- They listen to you.

- They give you honest advice to help navigate the pros and cons of a decision or situation.

- They are happy to see you become friends with other people.

- They steer you to be your best.

Best Friends Forever?

Many kids enjoy having close friends, and there is nothing wrong with that. But sometimes kids can get caught up in having a BFF. Their whole world revolves around that one person. But the term "best friend forever" shouldn't mean that you have to limit yourself when it comes to relationships with others. It shouldn't mean that your friends have to limit themselves to you, either.

One person can't possibly be everything to you, and you can't always be everything to someone else. That's a lot of pressure. Over time, people change and so do their interests. While it's wonderful to have that one friend you can always depend on, and grow and learn with, hanging out with other kids is important, too.

ARE YOU BEING A TRUE FRIEND?

Pick the best response to each situation below.

1. There's a new kid at school. During lunch, you want to introduce yourself to him. But your friend says, "We have enough friends. Why bother? Plus, I heard he's weird." You . . .

A) agree and stay where you are.

B) kindly say that you'd still like to meet him and head over to introduce yourself.

2. Your friend was just made captain of a team. She's really excited and wants to talk about nothing else. You . . .

A) gossip behind her back about how she always has to be the center of attention and doesn't really deserve to be captain.

B) tell her how happy you are for her and recognize the time and effort she put in to achieving her goal.

3. Your best friend just had a terrible fight with one of your other friends, but you are really focused on your upcoming vacation. You . . .

A) listen to her side of the story and offer positive advice.

B) interrupt her boring story to tell your exciting news.

4. You want to play tennis, but your friend wants to play roller hockey. She has a big tournament coming up and wants to be prepared. You . . .

A) call it a day and go your separate ways.

B) come up with a plan to spend some time playing both sports.

CHAPTER 4

Show You Care

....

Has anyone ever surprised you with a gift? What was it? How did it make you feel?

For Luke*, it was a small bag of pretzels at the right moment. He had just finished a rough day at elementary school. He had forgotten his homework, gotten in trouble for talking in class, failed a math test, and lost his favorite jacket. Nothing was going his way. When he got off the bus at the end of the school day, he trudged down the block to his home. His older brother, Peter*, was outside playing baseball with the rest of the neighborhood kids. Luke put his head down and kept walking. He knew his brother wouldn't let him play and if he asked, they would probably ignore him, call him annoying, or spend ten minutes debating which team he should be on because "he stinks."

But suddenly Peter ran up to him and put something in his hand. It was a small bag of pretzels. Peter said there was a snack sale at his school. He remembered that pretzels were Luke's favorite snack and bought them for him. Luke's face beamed. He couldn't believe it. Then Peter asked Luke to be on his team because they needed a decent pitcher.

"I pretty much forgot about the bad day I'd been having and ran to the house to grab my glove," says Luke.

Peter's thoughtful gift turned Luke's bad day around. It wasn't about the snack, though it was certainly a tasty treat. It was about the surprise, the unexpected positive attention from his brother.

According to a Gallup Poll, most people prefer surprise gifts. Expected gifts do fill our buckets, but for some reason, receiving things when we're *not* expecting them fills our buckets just a little more. Also, they are often the ones we remember the most. And the gift doesn't have to be anything big or expensive. It can be a gift of trust or responsibility. Sharing something personal or entrusting a friend with a secret can fill his or her bucket.

The key to great gift-giving is individualization. Each person is one of a kind, and has different likes and dislikes. What you might like, someone else might not. Some of us prefer tangible rewards or gifts. These are ones we can see, touch, and feel—and show off. Others are driven by words and acknowledgment. And while certain people want to receive praise in front of a crowd, others prefer a quieter, one-to-one compliment from someone they love, admire, or respect.

Look for opportunities to surprise your friends with small gifts—maybe a funny little toy or a kind word to let them know you're thinking of them. Even a smile can be a special gift. Consider unexpected sharing as well. Is there a book, photo, card, or drawing you could send someone that would give that person a boost?

Ways to Give Unexpectedly (And Make Your Thoughts Count)

- Give "bucket drops" or thank-you notes for things you notice or appreciate.

- Give your time. Spend time with someone who has been asking for your help, attention, or advice.

- Give by following through on your promises.

- Give by listening carefully and remembering the things other kids say that are important to them. Then act on something they mentioned.

- Give others credit for contributions they made to an activity you worked on together.

Putting praise into writing or a text is a wonderful gift, too. It's also rewarding because it serves as a lasting acknowledgment—something your friend can reflect on over and over again. And details make the difference.

When your praise is specific and sincere, your friends will know that you truly care about them.

For example, which praise or recognition would you prefer?

General praise: Nice painting.
Specific praise: Wow! I love the colors you used in your painting of the rain forest. That jaguar looks like it's about to jump off the canvas and eat me. You need to show me how to do that!

General praise: Good goal.
Specific praise: Your kick at the game yesterday was amazing. It flew over everyone's heads and right into the corner of the net. I hope I never have to goaltend against you!

General recognition: Here's your book back.
Specific recognition: Thank you so much for sharing your book with me. I was so worried that

I was going to mess up the assignment. You saved the day!

General recognition: Thanks.

Specific recognition: I'm so glad I have a friend like you to talk to. Thank you so much for listening. Your advice about being patient and practicing more really helped me solve my problem.

THE GIFTS THAT KEEP GIVING

On the lines below, write about some of the gifts you've received. Think about the impact these gifts had on you.

What is the greatest compliment you have ever received? Who gave it to you? When and where? Why was it special? How did it make you feel?

_____

_____

_____

_____

_____

_____

_____

_____

What is the most thoughtful gift you have ever received? Who gave it to you? When and where? Why was it memorable? How did it make you feel?

_____

_____

_____

_____

_____

_____

_____

_____

_____

_____

_____

_____

Have you ever received an unexpected gift? Who gave it to you? When and where? How did it make you feel? Why?

_____

_____

_____

_____

_____

_____

_____

_____

_____

_____

_____

_____

WRITE A DROP TO SOMEONE

Drops are handwritten, personal messages written on drop-shaped note cards. They're a simple way to share kind words with others, give unexpectedly, and fill someone's bucket.

Here's a challenge: Set a goal to write at least three bucket drops every month. Once you're done writing a drop, you can quietly slip the note to the recipient in person, send it, or read it out loud. Do whatever fills his or her bucket the most.

Name_____

_____

_____

_____

_____

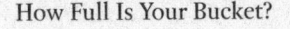

Name_____

_____

_____

_____

_____

_____

_____

_____

_____

_____

_____

_____

WRITE A DROP TO YOURSELF

While you're out bucket-filling, don't forget to fill your own bucket, too. Recognize and appreciate the good in you, and write a drop to yourself.

Name_____

_____

_____

_____

_____

_____

_____

_____

Name_____

_____

_____

_____

_____

_____

_____

_____

_____

_____

_____

_____

_____

Name_____

_____

_____

_____

_____

_____

_____

_____

_____

_____

_____

_____

_____

CHAPTER 5

Make a Difference

Ｈow many buckets can you fill in one day? A week? A month? Don't limit yourself. Go beyond your family, friends, and classmates. Think big, like Charlie.

In January 2015, Charlie and his family attended a professional basketball game at a local stadium. On the way home, Charlie spotted a homeless mother and her children huddled on the sidewalk. The experience left him heartbroken—but inspired. Charlie knew that Valentine's Day was coming up. It concerned him that people who are homeless probably don't have anyone to remember them on a holiday, especially one that is focused on love. So Charlie took action. He filled shoe boxes with water, food, socks, and supplies such as soap to give away to people in need. Charlie also decorated the boxes and included a handwritten Valentine's Day card in each one. His dad encouraged him to get some friends to help him and make it bigger.

Charlie's idea quickly spread. Several schools got involved and helped him make more than 300 boxes. Since then, the group, now known as Homeless at Heart, has expanded to other places. In 2018, its volunteers delivered more than 15,000 boxes in seven cities.

> *"It's important to appreciate what you have—and do what you can to help people," says Charlie.*

Charlie's not the only one filling buckets in his community and beyond. Paige is hard at work turning kids into "superheroes." She was born with a serious heart defect. Before Paige had an operation to fix the problem, she was seriously ill. Her mom made her a superhero cape while she was in the hospital. It made her feel stronger. Now she helps other sick kids feel that way. Paige and her mom started an organization called The Heart of Paige. They make superhero capes for kids in a local hospital. They hope the capes help young patients feel brave as they fight their illnesses.

> *"The kids are going through something hard. I try to keep smiles on their faces," says Paige.*

According to Gallup research, working to better your community helps boost your well-being and the well-being of others. (Well-being is the state of being happy and healthy.) Volunteering can give you a sense of purpose and meaning. It can also help you build relationships and provide you with a fresh outlook on life. We often get a sense of joy from giving a meaningful gift to a loved one, but perhaps no gift is as valuable as our time.

When Gallup asked happy and healthy people about the greatest contribution they had made in their life, most mentioned the impact they have had on another person, group, or community. Not only had they made a big contribution to something greater than themselves, but they also had been recognized for their community involvement. When we do things for others, we see how we can make a difference. This gives us confidence in our own ability to create change.

MY PLAN OF ACTION

What are some ways you can help people in your community? Write an idea for a volunteer project below.

Describe a problem facing people in your community:

_____

_____

_____

_____

_____

_____

_____

_____

_____

What are some ways in which people are already helping?

_____

_____

_____

_____

_____

_____

_____

_____

_____

_____

_____

_____

_____

What is another way you can help?

_____

_____

_____

_____

_____

_____

_____

_____

_____

_____

_____

_____

_____

Who could help you tackle the problem?

_____

_____

_____

_____

_____

_____

_____

_____

_____

_____

_____

_____

What will you call your team or organization?

_____

_____

_____

_____

_____

_____

_____

_____

_____

_____

_____

_____

_____

What resources will you need to solve this problem?

_____

_____

_____

_____

_____

_____

_____

_____

_____

_____

_____

_____

_____

MIND YOUR MINDSET

No matter how hard you try to fill buckets, sometimes you'll slip. Occasionally you may say things you'll regret and end up hurting someone's feelings. And no matter how hard you try to help others, your friends may sometimes leave you out.

At some point, you'll probably be teased for the clothes you wear, your hairstyle, and even your talents. You will not always get the best grade, be invited to the party, make the team, or win the game. You are going to make mistakes and occasionally be lonely. Often you'll feel that life is unfair. But you're not alone. These challenges face all of us.

When you're feeling down or facing a tough task, try to change the way you're talking to yourself. Take a deep breath and turn the negative sentences inside your head into positive ones. Here are some examples:

When Your Brain Says . . .	You Can Respond With . . .
This is too hard.	This may take some time and effort, but it's worth a try.
I'm not good at this.	Who can I ask for help? Who can help show me the way?
I give up.	There's one more thing I could do. And if not, hey, I tried my best. This just isn't for me.
How could I make such a stupid mistake?	Nobody's perfect. I will do my best to fix it and make it better. I will learn from this.
Nobody cares about me.	Yes, someone does. I may just need to reach out to them and ask for help, or allow them to help me when they do reach out.

Your responses to life's challenges matter. Knowing your strengths (yes, you have many!) and surrounding yourself with true friends will help you to survive them. Good friends can guide you in the face of loneliness and hard times. And remember, the world is a lot bigger than your home, neighborhood, or school. There are many more people to meet, opportunities to pursue, and places to explore beyond your front door. Seek out the positive, and you will thrive. Realize all of the amazing gifts you hold inside yourself and share them with the world. After all, you're a bucket-filler!

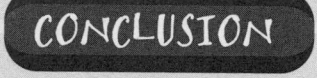

CONCLUSION

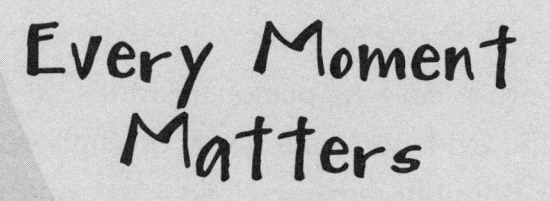

Every Moment Matters

. . . .

I magine what your world will be like one year after you have engaged in daily bucket-filling. We think the following changes may have occurred:

- Your school day will be a lot more fun.

- Your friendships will be stronger.

- You'll enjoy closer relationships with your family.

- You'll be healthier and happier.

There are plenty of personal stories—as well as scientific evidence—that show the importance of bucket-filling in our lives. Take every opportunity to increase the positive emotions of those around you. Practice bucket-filling with the people most important to you, like your parents, caretakers, or other family members. Tell them how important they are to you and why. Don't assume they already know. Even if they do, they'd probably love to hear it anyway. Continue to learn more about what builds them up and what brings them down.

It will make a big difference. It may even change the world.

Don't waste another opportunity.

Every moment matters.